THE ART OF MINDFULNESS

THE ART OF MINDFULNESS

Cultivating Awareness and Presence

SERAPHINA BLAKE

QuillQuest Publishers

CONTENTS

CHAPTER 1

Introduction to Mindfulness

Research shows that those who practice mindfulness actually change how the brain functions. As a result, it is harder to be "lost in thought," one can pay more attention to the moment and take in more information, and better cognitive skills emerge. However, this doesn't happen quickly. Mindfulness is not another "exercise program" for us to improve ourselves, although many people do feel calmer and more relaxed. Instead, mindfulness is about learning to be in the painful moments as well as in the more pleasant ones in your life. A good metaphor of mindfulness is when you go to the ocean and watch the waves, quietly, watching one wave come in, stay for a while, and then retreat. When you practice mindfulness, your thoughts might come and go throughout the practice, and that's fine. The point is to just bring the attention back to the breath when you notice that the mind has wandered.

In essence, mindfulness is about paying attention to our experiences, whether they are pleasant ("I bought a great piece of cake at the store today!") unpleasant ("Why do I have to work late all the time?"), or neutral ("I really need to get gas, and I hope this light doesn't turn red"). Most people do not pay much attention to their immediate experience, however. Instead, we often engage in many other activities besides what we are currently doing: thinking of the past or future, engaging in mental sorting or planning, daydreaming - the list of our distractions goes on and on. It is as though we are often on "automatic pilot", hardly aware of the present in our lives, perhaps even less of the people and world around us! Indeed, how often have we had entire conversations with others without our entire mind being there during the interaction? This is where mindfulness comes into play. With regular practice, we can learn to react or respond more deliberately, purposefully, and consciously, rather than habitually.

Definition and Origins of Mindfulness

This concept of "sati" was further built upon in the Buddha's discourses, forming what is known in Buddhism as "sati-mindfulness," or intentional/ethical mindfulness. Buddha believed that "sati" (remembrance) and "sampajano" (clear comprehension) helped keep one firmly grounded in the territory of the ethical by providing adequate attention to the future implications, as well as to the karmic results, of the actions performed. With this background, it is easy to draw connections between mindfulness and the Christian principles called for in the Sermon on the Mount. The idea of 'sati' is not restricted to Buddhism; traces of it are to be found in the Stoic tradition, where the 'practice of attention' is regarded as the psycho-ethical goal. In the West, this kind of awareness is closely related to "mindful awareness" as found in the humanistic psychotherapy of Carl Rogers (1976), where it refers to "the attitudes required to develop human qualities in full: attentive care, presence of mind, sensitivity to what is immediately present, willingness to understand, genuine interest."

What is mindfulness, and where does it come from? The term "mindfulness" appears in many texts related to self-improvement and meditation. But to gather a complete understanding of its meaning, we must look further back. The word mindfulness comes from the Pali word 'sati', which means "to remember." This root gives us the phrase "to put something in mind," or "right memory." While synonyms for mindfulness include "awareness" and "presence," it is important to note that its definition is "not simply being aware, but a certain kind of attention: an open, nonjudgmental attending." This broader meaning of the word "mindfulness" is important for understanding its origins and applications because it is a quality that can be a major factor in the reduction of stress, as well as in establishing one's emotional intelligence, or "intra-personal emotional process."

CHAPTER 2

The Benefits of Practicing Mindfulness

By engaging fully with the moment, we are far more open to the opportunities in front of us. By embracing a growth mindset and actively looking to learn from all sources, we also find ourselves unburdened by disappointment at our failures or setbacks, as they are seen as essential to the learning curve. Naturally, by embracing mindfulness in this way, and the accompanying presence and openness to growth, individuals often find themselves far more successful in every area of life - from career pursuits to relationships. By letting go of a rigid contentment with the present, we develop a deep relationship with the unfolding nature of all arenas of life and become highly attuned to novel ideas and opportunities that make for a fulfilled existence. It is therefore recommended that you undertake a mindfulness practice for at least 15 minutes per day in order to derive the maximum benefits.

Mindfulness puts our brains into a state of awareness, focus, and presence - assisting us to step out of autopilot mode and into an awakened, joyous existence. There is a multitude of health benefits associated with mindfulness, including: reduced symptoms of anxiety, depression, and other mental health conditions; improved attention, memory, and cognitive function; enhanced sleep; lowered blood pressure and heart rate. The act of being mindful can result in physical modifications to the size of brain structures, ultimately leading to the development of greater emotional regulation. Reduced activity in the amygdala allows for a slower processing of negative stimuli and a decrease in the generation of stress sensations, while increased activity in the pre-frontal cortex enhances our ability to be in control of emotions and behaviors. Serotonin and dopamine levels also become normalized, boosting our moods and elevating our overall sense of happiness - a direct result of regular mindfulness practice.

Physical Health Benefits

The first, most commonly studied claim for the effects of mindfulness on the body is its ability to affect the autonomic nervous system by reducing the stress of an individual. Activation of this system produces a myriad of physiological and mood changes (i.e., "fight or flight") and suppression allows for the restoration of biological functions (i.e., rest and digest). Mindfulness appears to be able to trigger the parasympathetic aspect of the nervous system, which is responsible for sleeping, digestion, etc. Another studied benefit of mindfulness is its ability to reduce chronic and acute pain. A third, less common benefit of mindfulness is its ability to regulate hormones such as cortisol, melatonin, or other hormone markers of stress. As noted by the studies presented, the majority of them have great difficulty finding a control group. Thus, due to this, most studies avoid randomization methodologies and rely on self-reported information.

While mindfulness and Mindfulness-Based Stress Reduction (MBSR) effectively reduce symptoms of depression or anxiety, the intent is to help increase awareness of the present. With that said, maintaining a quality of mental health through mindfulness practice can greatly decrease stress and a sense of feeling overwhelmed. In turn, these improvements in perceived mental well-being can also contribute to one's physical well-being. Not only is there considerable evidence to suggest that mindfulness and MBSR reduce stress, depression, and anxiety, but there is commensurate evidence to suggest that mindfulness has physical health benefits. For this reason, it is important to briefly discuss how mindfulness practice can affect different physical systems of the body.

Mental Health Benefits

Mindfulness might give you a more positive outlook on life. It captivates you with the grandeur and magnificence of the here and now. Not only can mindfulness help to improve your mood, it can teach you to let go of holding onto the negative. Anyone who experiences or thinks about pain and disability may agree that it will completely knock you off your balance. It might turn contentment and fulfillment into dust, too. Thankfully, there is growing research to suggest that mindfulness can improve an individual's ability to handle these life challenges. For example, one study highlighted that mindfulness lessened the emotional impact of everyday pain. Others have argued that by reducing the perception of pain, an individual may then feel more in charge of their pain and less likely to bother about it or let it control them. Therefore, you are less likely to experience emotional issues such as anxiety or depression because you become more physically and emotionally resilient, which is likely to affect your mental health positively.

So why all this fuss about mindfulness? What can 20 minutes, once a day, possibly do for you? The answer is: a lot. Firstly, and most obviously, mindfulness trains your attention; that is, you get better at focusing and observing. You are likely to have spent some time engaged in unproductive self-referential thinking, which is often in the form of worrying. Such rumination and excessive worrying leads to feelings of anxiety and depression. Spending more time focused on our immediate experience may reduce these mental health difficulties, and mindfulness does just this. A 2019 meta-analysis study conducted by Rezhetinskaya certainly showed that engaging in mindfulness was associated with reductions in anxiety, stress, and depression levels. Essentially, when chronically stressed, our nervous system becomes sensitized and can be set off into a panic response with little provocation. Mindfulness retrains the amygdala, which is the main alarm system of the body, reducing our panic reactions and enabling us to return to a state of emotional balance.

CHAPTER 3

Understanding the Science Behind Mindfulness

Various studies have revealed the neurological benefits of mindfulness. They explain it with sound scientific principles that appeal and make a person believe the effectiveness of practicing mindfulness. MRI scans of people who regularly practice mindfulness show a structurally different brain than those who don't. The practices produce changes in the brain that are associated with increased memory, attention, decision making, immune system function, emotional regulation, and vastly improved self-perception. Meditation has the power to literally raise your intelligence levels so that you can think, plan, and act with much more lucidity. Researchers have found that those who practice mindfulness can do so for longer periods because their brains begin to see the positive benefits of a clear head and mental wellness once the practice is undertaken. In addition to physical benefits, mindfulness has mental benefits. Existing studies have indicated that those who regularly practice it tend to have lower levels of stress, anxiety, and depression. Mindful children are less nervous and may also perform better in school because of their greater attention and comprehension.

Understanding the Science Behind Mindfulness

Wonder why the concept is in vogue and what exactly it entails? The art of mindfulness introduces practices that place attention on maintaining the present moment, cultivating awareness, and acceptance. But what is 'mindfulness', really? What happens to your brain when you practice mindfulness? Why does even modern medical science agree that practicing mindfulness every day is good for the body and soul?

Neurological Effects of Mindfulness

Because this kind of perspective and understanding of practice grounds and informs the sort of skills available, this text refers to different types of contemplative attention as virtue or ethical attention, aesthetic attention, and wisdom, or liberative attention. Simple awareness of these qualities of attention strengthens the insight and reduces confusion about the specifics of mindful contemplative practice. It also allows the integration of these practices with a burgeoning research base outside of studies traditionally classified as mindfulness research. Variations between practitioners and impacts also appear to evoke and track basic neurologically based aspects of human and animal affordance and attention systems. Neuroscience - Traditionally called the relationship between the nervous system and behavior, a fast and mostly automatic and unconscious set of signals. The brain can be reprogrammed to provide nuanced meaning systems of affordance, so identifying various ways of attention pays respect to attention's natural structures. Ethical attention activates systems for local sensations in time, more accurate perceptual discrimination instead of generalities.

• According to a 2018 article in the definitive journal, Nature Reviews Neuroscience, a growing body of neuroscience research shows that mindfulness actually changes both the function and structure of the brain in ways that other forms of relaxation cannot. • The umbrella term for these widely researched practices is also called contemplative practice. Orientation to the present moment, with acceptance, attention, and kindness evoked through the practices, reliably supports regenerative, integrative, and supportive mental and medical health benefits. Examples of these practices include meditation, prayer, and yoga. But recent research from the University of North Carolina shows the neurological impact, as well as the intensity of these strategies, differs. Cultivation of different qualities of attention appear to map onto different parts of the brain and support different forms of brain development.

CHAPTER 4

Key Principles of Mindfulness

The man had presumed that everybody should feel as he did. What the cashier was practicing is called mindfulness. This means being in a state of complete awareness. Mindfulness is coming to an understanding that even though the reality is unfortunate, we don't have to think of it as having to be negative. We can acknowledge the facts about the situation and, at the same time, understand our own response to them without feeling like the world is coming to an end. No matter what happens physically, we have choices about how we emotionally interpret the event of reality. Although morals are always preferred above falsities, it has been quoted that nothing worth mentioning can have a final ending, which brings us back to the story of the gloomy cashier, unable to go outside because of "bad" weather.

Out of the clear blue sky, the cashier says, "What a lovely day it is outside. I wish I could be out there where it's so warm and sunny." A man replies, "But it's cold and rainy outside. It's horrible." He knew the weather was bad just as well as the cashier. His reasons for arguing were that he hated rain and humidity and felt that everyone else should feel like him. The cashier smiled knowingly. She wasn't disappointed or angry; she was accepting the truth and the reality: It's cold and it's rainy.

Non-judgmental Awareness

Our observations represent a nonjudgmental awareness, which is an essential principle in any discussion of mindfulness. By non-judgment, we mean that we seek simply to observe. When we are practicing mindfulness, we allow our experiences to unfold, knowing that we cannot completely control this process. Instead, we open ourselves to what is happening, watching our thoughts, emotions, attitudes, and beliefs without judgment. We try to develop an attitude of curiosity and acceptance, drawing our focus over and over again to our breath, the experiences of our body, and the immediate world around us. We do not become distressed when we notice that our attention has wandered and begin to think about an unpleasant memory, a future event, and what other things we might connect to our thoughts.

Recognizing and accepting the bitter taste of coffee, the virtues in our friends along with their limitations, and the diversity, energy, and beauty in the world that surrounds us are all acts of mindfulness. Each is a distinct step on the continuum between a life led carelessly on automatic pilot and one discovered through being fully and actively here now, to no one moment more than another. Notice that on the continuum between living on autopilot and being in the moment, nowhere is judgment considered. This is because our job as observers of our life is simply to observe without judgment of the experiences that arise.

CHAPTER 5

Mindfulness Practices

Basic Practices and Exercises: The following is a list of some of the fundamental mindfulness practices. Of course, a different exercise might be modified to include a formal structure and for our purposes be seen as a practice in mindfulness. These exercises and practices were chosen more for their ease and accessibility as basic forms of mindfulness that can be performed in a regular way. It is our hope that you will use and be creative with them, turning everyday situations into those that serve you on your journey of being mindful. - Being with the Breath - Spacious Attention - Expanding the Attention: Essentially means to increase its power, or in other words, to become more aware of consciousness itself. It is more the removal of any object of perception, and the allowing of the natural state, free from grasping or complications. - Mindful Walking - Stress Reduction - A Mindfulness Eating Exercise - A Relaxed Attitude - Mindfulness While Formally Sitting.

1. Body Scan: As you attend to your breath, attend to your body's sensations, noticing areas of comfort, discomfort, and neutrality. 2. Mindfulness of Breath: Observe the breath, letting it be just as it is, and simply see what happens. Some suggested practices include counting breaths, tagging thoughts, noting the ebb and flow of the breath, or meditating on lovingkindness or

compassion while focusing on each breath. 3. Walking Meditation: Practice mindfulness during walking. 4. Kindly Awareness: Attend to qualities such as thought, feeling, or visual experience through patience, acceptance, openness, and other heart-based attitudes. 5. Mindfulness of Thinking: Observe thought, language, and imagination. 6. Mindfulness of Emotions: Perceive and learn from emotional tones and nuances. 7. Fresh Royalty: Accompany the novelty of experiences invited by beginner's mind. 8. Mindfulness of Silence: Recognize unknown aspects of speech, perception, and self.

Breath Awareness Meditation

Let's give it a try. Having prepared yourself by sitting comfortably, begin by taking a few breaths. Are they shallow or deep, even or gasping? For now, just notice. As you inhale, follow the breath from the moment it enters your nostrils and be present with it as it travels down into your lungs, and then follow it as it travels up and out of your nostrils. Is it warm or cool? Notice if it travels through to your throat as well. Resist the urge to manipulate or change the breath, simply pay attention. Can you extend the breath, making it deeper and slower without straining? What does it feel like if you make the out breath longer than the in breath? After this simple inventory, do not attempt to judge or categorize, simply observe. Allow your breath to return to its natural equilibrium and let your entire focus now be in watching the breath as it moves in and out of your body. Watch as though it were someone else's breath, something neutral, uninvolved with your emotions or opinions. Likely, the longer you watch, the more profound the shift from the conscious focus of inhalation and exhalation, and you will notice a gentle ebbing and flowing movement of the breath itself. Breathe and relax into the stillness within the space of the in-between!

Our breath is the anchor to which we tether our mind's linear capacity so that we can access the vastness of our inner being. One of the most readily available tools of returning to the present moment is to become aware of the in and out rhythm of your own breath. This deceptively simple tool is invaluable. You may feel you have breath so mastered that it can progress quite happily without you needing to dull your blades of attention. Yet, because our breath is rhythmic, it offers a great point of focus that allows us to experience a going deep inside ourselves, away from the demands of the exterior world.

CHAPTER 6

Incorporating Mindfulness into Daily Life

Homemakers can benefit by intentionally focusing on their tasks, such as dusting, vacuuming, or sorting mail, rather than allowing their minds to wander. The car can be a place to practice mindfulness as well. Driving can be done with full awareness of its every aspect, such as putting on your blinker and observing traffic patterns around you, and monitoring changes in such patterns even when you are sitting at a long stoplight. As part of cultivating non-judging and a non-striving mind state, cultivate an awareness of the rewards of those choices that contain their own pleasure or joy, no matter how small, such as feeling more peaceful with a less-cluttered house and eating in a more balanced manner.

Living mindfully doesn't just happen when you're sitting in meditation, but also when you're engaged in everyday activities. As with any new skill, integrating mindfulness into your day takes time and practice. Below are many suggestions for extending mindfulness from the meditation cushion into your daily life. Select one suggestion at a time that you can imagine yourself applying for a full week, then another for another week. Choose practices that are a good fit for your personality and lifestyle, and work up to incorporating mindfulness into as many of your daily activities as possible.

Mindful Eating

You can try to eat to live happily and practice with each meal. The practice will not be effective if you do not usually adopt it. People eat while watching television or discussing business. They don't know what they are eating, but doctors say that if you use a new drug and you are not sure, it will not work. This is not a regular practice. Regular practice must be improved step by step. Just as running laps or skipping every day - and adding more and more next to it, you will have new energy to run. We need to train our body and mind according to the Buddhist tradition in order to benefit entirely from the full effects of consumption. As previously stated, it is critical in our experience. Regular training will help the practitioner develop his or her attentiveness and recognize the true quality of the food. If we stop eating without fully appreciating the food, we will not have the real nutrients.

Eating is, in and of itself, a meditation practice. People eat for a variety of reasons, but those who practice this form of eating do so to nourish their body and generate happiness and joy in the present moment. Other purposes for eating, in their view, such as relieving stress, disrupting loneliness, or checking a certain dish off a must-eat-while-in-the-City restaurant, channel our attention away from the simple joy of eating. Eating is one of the most important daily acts. It's a pity that we spend so little time to do it in perfect condition. Drinking a cup of tea, waiting for 2 minutes to rinse the parts, to enjoy each second. It is wonderful.

CHAPTER 7

Cultivating Presence and Awareness

People who are not present can most usually describe that their thoughts are floating away in the future, overanalyzing what is coming and predicting how it will come about or what might go wrong. Another way to train yourself in being present is to use sensory awareness and focusing on the five senses: touch, sight, taste, sound and scent. This is a good exercise when we think of being present, as the five senses are always in the present. This is a good way to remind yourself to come back to the present moment. Lastly, it is important to remember that the practice of mindfulness is a skill and, as with anything, it takes time to learn. Be patient and remember the more you practice mindfulness, the more healing will occur in your life.

One of the central facets of mindfulness is the development of present-moment awareness. There are several ways to enhance this awareness in our everyday lives. One is to focus on using intention. Simply intend to be present. It takes a change of mindset, recognizing and acknowledging the present moment as a unique experience. And then remind yourself to come back to the present moment once that experience is over. It could be the realization that those moments are already long gone. Another way of getting in touch with the present moment is to focus awareness on the way our bodies feel. People often say that focusing on physical sensation helps them reconnect with the here and now.

Being Present in the Moment

Practicing as if Everything Matters It is important to approach the practice as a particular endeavor or task rather than a "special" type of experience that we create; however, we can generate this sense of relative importance by generating an attitude that what we attend to is important in the moment. Generally, it is our judgments and expectations of what matters or is important that clutter up the "moment-to-moment" nature of our attending. As we develop the ability to attend to objects directly and with a positive attitude, we vacate the mind's "less important" concerns and escape the trap of outcome orientation. A sense of presence will grow and deepen autogenically.

Abiding in Presence: A Strategy You might find it helpful to request, "May my attention be gently guided to the activities and objects of this current moment." Cultivate the idea that your activities – whether they are directly experienced as pleasant, unpleasant, or neutral – are worthy objects of your present moment attention. As you go about your activities, repeatedly express an intention to yourself to keep your attention anchored simply in what you are currently doing. Let your body and immediate sensory experience guide you. That is, if you are washing the dishes, tune into the movements of your arms, hands, etc., the temperature and pressure of the water, the smell and sight, etc.

Cultivating awareness of the present moment is an important aspect of mindfulness practice; this is also sometimes equated with keeping our attention anchored in immediate sensory experience, i.e., "be here now!" This is an important skill to develop, especially in a society rife with imperatives that encourage "doing" over simple "being." In this section, we describe practical strategies to move our focus away from habitual thoughts about the past or future, giving some freedom from these self-perpetuating thoughts.

CHAPTER 8

Mindfulness in Different Contexts

Those that are familiar with optical illusions know that by deliberately changing our perception of something, we change our experience. Mindfulness can deepen these moments - and also make an impact when life seems intolerable. Mindfulness, in its various forms, is a deliberate awareness of whatever is happening in the present moment. It is a way of enhancing protection from stress and depression. Mindfulness is a form of mental fitness. It is a way of building capacity to bring our attention to ourselves and to our surroundings in a particular manner - on purpose, in the moment, and non-judgmentally. All mindfulness practices teach the development of an ability to attend closely to whatever we are experiencing internally or in the world around us. Through this regular practice, the 'object' of our attention broadens. It includes all zones of emotional and physical well-being, leading to a renewed focus upon relationship, productive activity, well-being, spirituality and capacity. Mindfulness has been shown to lead to happier, more ethical, more effective leadership and greater capacity for innovation. In fact, it is an essential component of effective leadership in the 21st century.

• Mindfulness at schools is delivered in an age-appropriate way. Mindfulness for students is called various names like 'feeling stronger'.

• Mindfulness in healthcare is also called mindfulness-based stress reduction or mindfulness-based cognitive therapy. There is also a special mindfulness practice described to support those suffering from cancer. • For people facing chronic health difficulties, tailored mindfulness courses are also available. These include mindfulness for cardiac failure, PTSD and disordered/dysfunctional eating. • In the workplace there are courses called 'mindfulness-based resilience training', 'mindfulness for compassionate perceived stress in the helping industries'. There is even a course in Denmark called 'mindfulness for police officers'. • There is an intervention for the US military (specifically veterans) called 'mindfulness-based wellness and resilience'. There are also tailored interventions for mindfulness in the legal profession and for organizational leaders. • While there are mindfulness programs for the criminal justice system and the detention system, there are also various interventions in meditation and yoga for people in prison or detention. • There are also tailored mindfulness interventions for parents such as 'mindful parenting' and 'mindful star of hope'. • When it comes to caring for the self, mindfulness can be used with informal mindfulness practice or more formally with sitting meditation instruction. There are mindful eating programs, mindful recovery groups and programs for kids: 'mindfulness in a jar'.

Mindfulness in the Workplace

Some of the inspiration and teachings found in the practice of mindfulness, whether it be in the context of a psychotherapeutic relationship or through the teachings of the world's religious traditions, are relevant to the workplace. Work organizations can be large and complex groups of people, often possessing a collective culture and history that is hidden until one becomes immersed within its social and cultural life. The purpose of organizations can be as diverse as the people who work within them, and in the contemporary world, the pressure to increase profitability at any cost can lead to exploitation of human and environmental resources and result in products and services that mirror the negative and exploitative values of the organizations that manufacture them. However, organizations are also capable of doing much good in the world, and organizations are constituted of individuals who contribute a vital and living force to their psychic and social reality. Our values, assumptions, hopes, and fears are part of the cultural web that individuals are enmeshed in. Mindfulness invites individuals to turn towards this complex social and psychic reality with awareness and presence. Through taking the time to notice what is happening and to seek to become free of the unacknowledged forces that operate inside the human heart, expensive and destructive internal politics that are often played out in the workplace can be gradually reduced in their crippling effect. It seems appropriate then, in the spirit of the teachings of mindfulness, to also examine some of the qualities, insights, and pathologies of the workplace better to understand and promote a more positive work experience.

The boom of mindfulness is largely based upon the use of it as a psychotherapeutic tool, and the techniques and understanding that have been developed as a result of this work are informing the rekindling of interest in the deep and diverse streams of knowledge and wisdom upon which mindfulness first drew. However, just as the individualistic bias of psychotherapy is giving way to embracing frameworks for understanding emotional and relational distress that draw upon a socio-political and ecological vision of human nature, so too is this informing contemporary versions of meditation practice.

CHAPTER 9

Overcoming Common Challenges in Mindfulness Practice

In this way, the practice of meditation mirrors the practice of life. So, that's another difficulty. We might feel we don't have time to meditate or be mindful. And isn't it too self-indulgent? What about the fast pace of life? All of these can feel enough to put you off practicing mindfulness. But being more aware can help you face these challenges, and to meet the range of difficulties many people have in their practice, I've devised a number of practices and strategies to bring your curiosity and warmth to the experience as well as the discipline of mindfulness itself. With regular effort over time, you will find you slow down, feel more chilled, and can respond more skillfully to difficulty.

Mindfulness practice is simple, but it isn't easy. Here are some strategies and insights that will help you navigate common obstacles and come out better for it. There are several ways we experience obstacles when we practice mindfulness. The first way is to believe we are the only one struggling, that everyone else is calm and peaceful, and that there is something wrong with us for finding it challenging. That's not the case. Sure, some people may relish sitting in silence, feeling their breaths. But many of us have difficulty. We feel restless or bored. We think a lot. And it's difficult to find some comfortable meditation position. We find it hard not to react to every thought that comes into his head, difficult to stop ourselves from judging our difficulty and getting angry, or writing lists in our minds and suddenly recalling past hurts and believing we are no good and never will be.

Dealing with Distractions

Paying purposeful attention to oneself in a particular way and on purpose invites awareness and presence into our lives. There are many distractions that take us to a less balanced and integrated place in a world that moves quickly and is full of constant change. If we can become aware of some of these distractions and if we can pay attention to how this information translates throughout our 5 dimensions, we can begin to refine our mind-body-behavior-soul integration.

Mindfulness serves as a tool to focus our attention, and over time, this ability to concentrate or broaden our focus enhances our ability to regulate and control our emotions. Through mindfulness, you can increase your ability to ignore negative stimuli and manage stress.

Pondering approach. If you keep getting pulled away from your practice by some kind of problem or situation that you are facing, maybe thinking about it would give you a feeling of relief about not facing it. Think for about one minute while doing nothing else before returning to your practice. Most of the deliberation approach is the same as the other two approaches, but the thought is used for relief rather than letting go.

Letting go. Rather than labeling or using your breath to let go of the unwanted thought, emotion, note the event and use your breath to let go of the tension that comes with holding onto unhelpful thoughts, emotions. Each time it arises, note it, acknowledge it, watch, and then let go. Approach it like a leaf landing on a stream, floating along, and then floats away.

Labeling approach. When a distracting thought, emotion, or sensation pops up, notice it, label it as "thinking" - and this can work for other mental projects, such as worrying, fantasizing, and replaying an incident. Touch or lightly note your thought and then return focus to your primary focus.

CHAPTER 10

The Role of Mindfulness in Emotional Regulation

The emotions, or more critically, how people manage and regulate them, have long been of interest to people. Emotion regulation is now well established as a critical process in psychological well-being and a range of psychological disorders. In this body of work, the authors seek to further elucidate the mechanisms by which mindfulness influences the management and regulation of emotion. The guest editor will briefly introduce the content of all papers in the issue and provide an overarching theoretical framework to guide a read-through of the special issue. They motivate a theoretical approach drawing from classical psychology and mindfulness traditions and use clinical and laboratory-based research articles to unpack the core themes outlined in this article. They suggest that mindfulness may facilitate two domains of emotional functioning, each a pivotal stage in the process of emotion regulation: (1) increasing the level of metacognitive-affective awareness required in order to identify emotions at earlier and subtler stages of processing and (2) enhancing emotional tolerance for aversive states, possibly via processes of exposure and eventual extinction.

Over recent decades, there has been growing interest in the scientific study of mindfulness. A large body of research now attests to the benefits of mindfulness practice across various domains including health, psychological well-being, and interpersonal relationships. Multiple, interrelated cognitive, affective, and neural mechanisms underpinning these benefits have been elucidated. This paper presents a collection of interrelated articles examining the evidence for these mechanisms with a focus on the role of mindfulness in emotion regulation.

Managing Stress with Mindfulness

There are several concepts related to mindfulness that research has found to be particularly effective for stress management; many of these will sound familiar as they have been discussed earlier in the book. For instance, labeling one's negative emotions (e.g., "feelings of anger," "feelings of sadness") has been shown to reduce brain activity in the limbic area related to fear and emotions. In addition, training in mindfulness practice that involves observing one's breath or saying the word "Om" in a systematic way results in a cumulative reduction in the level of perceived stress. One basic form of mindfulness meditation involves simply observing the natural flow of one's breath in and out for ten to twenty minutes. Non-violent prayer has a similar effect and is associated with increased subjective measures of calmness as well as physiological signs of relaxation. Further, activities that promote rest and relaxation, such as drumming, may also have a calming and centering effect when incorporated into spiritual practices. The exercise that we will look at next asks readers to harness these concepts to combat stress.

Stressful experiences can be a common part of life, and sometimes they are so common that we forget how often we dislike or struggle through them. In our daily lives, when we react to relatively small stressors with intense irritation or by pulling away, we can be sure that many stressful experiences have not been acknowledged for what they are – stress. One of the best things about mindfulness is that regardless of the intensity of the stress, we can start right now and in any moment to reduce its power and expand our skills related to it.

CHAPTER 11

The Intersection of Mindfulness and Compassion

Mindfulness, in not being judgmental, provides understanding and patience, making it a fertile resource for the development of compassion. Over time, growth in self-kindness, accumulated from mindfulness practice, leads to a more positive self-view. This in turn makes it easier to work with the self-judgments and self-criticism that stifle compassion, which is easier because mindfulness helps reduce rumination and makes it easier to let go of self-criticism. Compassion is traditionally seen as a practice accomplished through meditation to develop love and kindness: extending compassion to oneself, extending compassion to friends and all beings, and extending to all beings everywhere. Emotionally speaking, it is easier to feel compassion for a filly than for a stranger, so the effect is in decreasing the effective size of the community of our compassionate concern and increasing the effective size of the community of our compassionate concern. We can expand its scope by moving on to identify us as friends and ultimately identifying the enemies in common with our compassionate concern. Conducting compassion meditation has been related to prosocial behavior. It eventually becomes natural to be compassionate to everyone, even if we do a simple act like smiling or exchanging "hello" with others.

The art of mindfulness and the practice of compassion go hand in hand. Expanding our perspective allows us to embrace all sides of who we are, including those aspects from which we may momentarily shrink. When we practice compassion and soften our resistance to our own suffering, something profound happens: We begin to understand that we are not alone in pain. Our difficulties are part of a shared human life. There is a natural and strong connection between mindfulness and compassion. Mindfulness helps people cope with stress, anxiety, and depression and can improve self-awareness. Although the initial focus of mindfulness meditation practice is often self-awareness, mindfulness is more than self-awareness or monitoring of internal processes. Jack Kornfield, the renowned mindfulness teacher who is a father in the American mindfulness movement, once said, "If you want to be mindful, begin by being kind to yourself."

Self-Compassion Practices

Self-Compassion Break: This brief, informal practice has three parts and can be done almost anywhere. First, call to mind a situation in your life that is causing you stress. Call up the emotions connected with it and then say to yourself: "This is a moment of suffering." Next, say to yourself: "Suffering is a part of life." This is about feeling connected to everyone who suffers, "the shared human condition," and is a way of putting our suffering into perspective. Then, put your hands over your heart, feel your hands warm your chest area as you say to yourself, "May I be kind to myself." You can then continue to practice other self-compassion exercises or return to what you were doing before.

Compassion Meditation: Attune to the suffering in your body, heart, or mind. You might find it helpful to recall specific illness-related stressors that have recently led to feelings of pain, hurt, fear, or sadness. Don't push too hard. Try focusing on your heart area or your breath, and on each in-breath, imagine receiving compassion from others. On each out-breath, extend a sense of warmth and caring to yourself.

Compassion and Self-Compassion Practices: While the previous loving-kindness practices invite a kind, nurturing stance toward oneself, these practices are specifically designed to soften identifications with experiences of suffering and illness, which is especially relevant when dealing with illness and disease.

A practice of simply bringing oneself to mind, evoking a sense of warmth and tenderness toward oneself, can follow an established metta meditation practice.

Metta (Loving-Kindness) Meditation: Here, numerous phrases are used in a mantra-like way to direct well-wishes toward people. We are working on cultivating an attitude of warmth and friendliness toward ourselves by imagining ourselves as the recipient of our own well-wishes. This formal meditation is often done in a progressive way, where one moves through a sequence of extending well wishes to an increasing circle of people, beginning with oneself and moving outward until one extends well-wishes to all beings.

Loving-Kindness Series: These practices—particularly the first two—can cultivate a more loving, self-nurturing view of ourselves and an understanding of how to direct well-wishes to oneself.

CHAPTER 12

Cultural and Historical Perspectives on Mindfulness

A pragmatic classification of mindfulness in terms of tradition and culture includes Eastern meditation, MBSR, Vipassana, TM, Mantra, Kinhin, Shamatha, Tsa-lung, Chenrezig, Dzog-chhen, Mahamudra, Rigpa, Zen, Buddha-nature, Dzogchen, Pamojjo, Insight, Samadhi, Bhorano, Anekajati, Patisotagami, Law of Attraction, Mahabodhi, the Four Foundations of Mindfulness, Mindfulness-Based Compassionate Living for All, MBSR, MBCT, and so on.

The ethical and cultural roots of mindfulness and its cultivation of bare attention are found in tradition. It has been practiced as a structured meditation technique during the last centuries. Mindfulness has been considered the first step of the Noble Eightfold Path and an important policy of culture, philosophy of life, mental training, and healthy living based on the movement of Buddhist teaching. Regardless of the fundamentals of cultural and historical aspects, religions and philosophies, mindfulness has been defined widely and classified into several types in terms of its tradition, culture, and practicability.

Mindfulness practices have long been part of human history, yet they are often unknown or misunderstood. Sometimes their origins are confused with those of other practices like meditation and relaxation techniques. Mindfulness practices do not belong to a specific religion, philosophy, or culture. They focus on promoting a particular state of consciousness, irrespective of time and place. Knowing the origins and culture of mindfulness can contribute to a better understanding of the terminology and history of the phenomena related to this. There also exist different manifestations of the concept and practice of mindfulness. Despite this cultural and historical background, mindfulness practices do not belong to a specific tradition. We can find evidence of practices that are very similar to this topic in different religious, spiritual, and philosophical traditions, as well as in different human cultures.

Mindfulness in Eastern Traditions

At the heart of the modern tradition of mindfulness, and much of the material within Western thought, is the set of texts called the Pali Canon. These texts outline a broad framework for understanding human consciousness and mindfulness. As such, several scholars and translators of Pali have sought to recast the Western discourse of mindfulness into the Eastern philosophical framework from which they are understood. Understanding this framework will not only have a profound influence on understanding what the core practices of mindfulness ought to look like but will also imbue the entire subject of mindfulness with the profound historical weight that is often lacking in Western renditions.

For thousands of years, the East has been home to rich traditions of mindfulness that extend from the Hindu traditions of ancient India to the classical Buddhist practitioners and texts of the third century BCE. This deep cultural and philosophical heritage is the bedrock of the modern mindfulness movement, extending from the mid-20th-century work of such scholars as Jon Kabat-Zinn, a former student at the Zen Center of San Francisco, who predominantly draws from the teachings of Soto Zen Master Taisen Deshimaru.

CHAPTER 13

The Evolution of Mindfulness in Western Society

Millennia of crossing and fusing belief on the Indian subcontinent have produced philosophies rich in contradiction and antinomy. However, while there is a long Tantra/Chan/Zen/Dzogchen tradition of apophatic or paradoxical teaching, meditation/awareness training does remain an organizing feature of Eastern methods known as 'mindfulness' training in the contemporary Western world. Indeed, the West has had, in recent years, a sustained, military, political, corporate, and healthcare-based discussion on employing mindfulness training techniques to manage soldiers' stress and improve their fighting potential. Furthermore, the United States Defense forces are investigating ancient Hindu 'Yoga' as a way to prepare soldiers for the stress of modern conflict. These developments in the West are particularly interesting in the increasing synergy between acts, international and state law, and spirit orientalism in official military space.

The practice of mindfulness has been evolving in various forms for thousands of years and is fundamental to virtually all of the world's religious and spiritual traditions. It has only very recently come into wider application, corporate, or business settings, or for the treatment of mental health issues. Indeed, the application of traditional mindfulness activities, for instance, eating, walking, or breathing, is considered a radical transformation that farmers and yogis, not project managers, undertake at their weekend getaways. It is worth noting that in all of these conceptualizations, certain modifications have been made in the name of cultural integration and capture academic audiences. According to some, this is a simple repackaging of a time-worn therapy. A stated aim of this thesis is to investigate whether such criticisms have merit.

Integration into Psychology and Therapy

More or less contemporary with the growth of cognitive therapy, a flow of literature on mindfulness proper has emerged in the West, several of these writings available in English, as well as some journals and books. A striking feature of this modern interest in mindfulness is what Leiberg and Roth (1998) describe as the 'psychologizing of mindfulness' within the sphere of self-help books. Some 14 have been identified to date, most of them published within the last five years. Leiberg and Roth suggest that if mindfulness begins to enjoy a degree of authority, it is because such authority bonuses it by the fact that it has been incorporated into psychological practices in the West as 'positive thinking'. The interest within the psychological is, according to the authors, an industrial interest - the all-mindfulness company. The introduction of mindfulness-based meditation techniques in therapy is already occurring in the United Kingdom, though very few cases have been assembled. Concentrating on the psychology journals, the integration of mindfulness within psychology represented below is taken from Psyndex and abstracts. Few of the articles actually refer to Kabat-Zinn, and none of the articles has it as their subject. In the UK, mindfulness playing a part in psychology enjoys middle-class popularity among a small public sector elite, and, it would seem, some academic and health-care professionals.

Beginning with the mindfulness practices of Kabat-Zinn (1990), the early 1980s saw the first introduction of mindfulness within the arena of Western psychology. Within the United Kingdom, therapists then began incorporating aspects of mindfulness within techniques labelled cognitive therapy. The emphasis is not, as in mindfulness proper, on 'living in the moment' but rather on non-evaluative attention to present-moment experience. Various authors have drawn from the approach including Varey, Harper, and Teasdale. Varey's work utilises an 'objective detachment from discursive processes' such that one disengages from belief in the content of thoughts and the associated discomfort. Harper more specifically draws explicit attention to the concept of mindfulness, indicating that cognitive therapy provides 'mindfulness-based cognitive therapy' (MBCT) available in Harper. It frankly acknowledges its association with Buddhism. Teasdale is, of course, the co-author of the book attractive to so many, although he does not draw directly on the 'therapeutic aspects of Buddhist psychology' within the work. In contrast, Segal has originated and encouraged development of MBCT courses at Toronto University, focusing specifically on mindfulness itself rather than the cognitive aspects.

CHAPTER 14

Mindfulness and Ethical Considerations

Such an exercise can also be carried over to the practice of mindfulness more generally. What is the present state of my ethical or moral values and how might they be supporting or conflicting with the practice of mindfulness? Drawing our attention to the present also draws attention to the ethical admonitions regarding how the present moment may be steered. What responsibility do we bear for the kinds of world that our individual attention participates in creating and sustaining? As we make abiding structural changes in our perception made possible by the practice of mindfulness, so we begin to change the world. As the world changes, so too does the practitioner, in a dependent origination of practice and ethics. An ethical posture to mindfulness begins not just with being aware but also with being in right relation to what is present.

Mindfulness is not neutral or value-free. It is important for a practitioner, whether or not they identify as Buddhist, to be aware of and make ethical considerations in the practice of mindfulness. Since mindfulness draws our attention to the present moment, the practice of it might have the ethical implication of potentially leading us to be more ethical individuals. A first step might be reflecting on the present state of our attention, how "on" we are or how distracted, what we are focusing on and how it feels.

Ethical Implications of Mindfulness Practice

One way to facilitate philosophical contemplation is by asking philosophical questions. An ethical question asks directly about the course of action an individual chooses. Other things equal, from all the options we entertain, the one we dethrone through our active decision by actually selecting it would be the most we could do, the most we could be. Can we contemplate our decision as such? Can we slow thought down enough to deliberate actively? The first decision seems to me to animate otherwise the flickering energy of brief flicks of formulation and pastiche these first two questions.

Ethical dilemmas pervade contemporary psychotherapy. It is important to take a step back from contentious debates regarding appropriate professional relationship boundaries, the place of religious and spiritual concerns in therapeutic endeavors, and the potential risks associated with borrowing practices from divergent contemplative traditions, in an effort to consider mindful practice with some distance. What in this way of doing is ethical or unethical? Clearly, from the perspective of virtue theory, what is meant by ethical implicates the intentions and dispositions of individuals. It is not an issue of legal or professional obligation. Thus, virtue theory is more direct in focusing our attention on the loaded question, "What kind of person are you?" Given the specific ethical aim of this book, it is important to explore mindful practice with the question "What kind of person do you want to become?" in mind.

CHAPTER 15

The Future of Mindfulness Research and Applications

Ethical Considerations and the Role of Mindfulness. Many scholars have suggested that mindfulness research should take into consideration the ethical role of these practices, how they can possibly lead to abuse, and the need for purchasing them under certain ethical guidelines. In particular, it has been suggested that we should be more cautious in applying secular terms and, in general, the idea of taking a practice out of the tradition it comes from and transposing it into another context. While other researchers have pointed out the difficulty of disentangling ethical from theoretical issues, new frameworks looking to serious ethical considerations of practice are likely to emerge.

Developing Contemplative Science. An emerging direction is in the area of developing a contemplative science framework. In this model, rather than conducting separate research that identifies problems and then tinkers with solutions, the science would be conceived to engage with the practice in a way that is truly responsive to and in cooperation with the practice itself. This would involve working closely with experts, above all the practice community themselves, and designing the research according to pressing needs and questions rather than simple factors of novelty, utility, or feasibility. It might also lead to directing studies to target the multiplier effects in factors of practice transmission and sharing.

Emerging Trends in Mindfulness Studies

Indeed, as we peer into the future of the field, we also find that mindfulness is increasingly being tested as a tool in a variety of unique, novel and pressing contexts. We have highlighted several of these in the present volume, such as the potential role of mindfulness in helping patients, families and other health care workers cope with the stress of coping with disease today; the way in which mindfulness and modifications of mindfulness training paradigms might potentially play a role in influencing the electorate and thus the nature and quality of our very democracy; how meditative techniques that are at some level similar to mindfulness (although often not called that) can help to elucidate the basic principles of human learning and memory; and the way in which individuals and institutions increasingly seek out mindfulness as a tool for moral and emotional self-examination, for skillful and wise ethical decision making, and for dealing with diversity and inclusion in our corporate and institutional environments.

For the first 15 years of the 21st century, hundreds of articles on the science of mindfulness were published. Given the size of a typical research article, we estimate that more than a million words on mindfulness have been published every month in peer-reviewed journals since 2000. If the boom in mindfulness starts to ebb or plateau in the near future, as fashions often do, then we still have an overwhelming synthesis of findings to review and organize. However, we are heartened by the evidence of a number of substantive advances emerging from the deeply productive and reflective cutting edge of the field. In this subsection, we highlight some of these recent trends to provide readers with an idea of the direction the field might take in the coming years. Our selections are by no means exhaustive, but we believe they are illustrative of the kinds of emerging topics, as yet fresh and half formed, that researchers and practitioners increasingly turn their attention to going forward.